The Battle for Europe

*Commentary on Acts
7, 12, 13, 14, 15, 16, 17 & 18*

K.W. Bow

Copyright 2016 by Kenneth W. Bow
The book author retains sole copyright to his contributions to this book.
Published 2016.
Printed in the United States of America.

All rights reserved.

No portion of this book may be reproduced, stored in a retrieval system, or transmitted in any form or by any means – electronic, mechanical, photocopy, recording, scanning, or other – except for brief quotations in critical reviews or articles, without the prior written permission of the author.

ISBN 978-1-9860028-7-8

Front cover design by Mark Gauthier.

This book was published by BookCrafters,
Parker, Colorado.
bookcrafterscolorado@gmail.com

This book may be ordered from
www.bookcrafters.net and other online bookstores.

Foreword

I treasure the friendship and ministry of Doctor Kenneth Bow as one of God's most precious gifts to me.

For Forty years God has used him to bless His Kingdom and feed His people with the finest of the wheat.

Like Joshua the High Priest, he is among those men wondered at.

(Zech 3:8 Hear now, O Joshua the high priest, thou, and thy fellows that sit before thee: for they are men wondered at:)

Pastor Bow is revered by his generation, as a hero of the faith, a champion of truth, and preacher most beloved.

Not only is he my favorite preacher, but my hero as well. His ministry is without equal and as a writer he has no peer.

God has graced him with great understanding, wisdom, and anointing. Reading his books makes one feel as if they were reading the writings of the Apostle Paul. His Solomon-like wisdom shines through with amazing insight on every scripture.

You will love everything this man writes. Read and be blessed!

Martyn Ballestero

Chapter 7

7.1 Then said the high priest, Are these things so?

7.1 Stephen is Stephanos, a garland or crown, in the Greek language. Garlands or crowns were given by the ancient Greeks to those who rendered good services to their cities, or brought fame to them by winning triumphs. Stephen was to win in this chapter an imperishable garland, and to gain a crown of righteousness. The previous persecutions of the church had been raised by the Sadducees, but this time it was the Grecian Jews. The Libertines had been slaves, Jewish captives, taken in the various wars waged by the Romans. They had been dispersed among the Romans at Rome and elsewhere. There in their captivity they had learned the Greek language and become acquainted with Greek culture; and now, when they had recovered their freedom they returned to Jerusalem in such numbers that a synagogue of the Libertines was formed. These were the people who opposed Stephen. The High Priest here was probably Theophilus, son-in-law of Caiaphas. It is believed by some it was actually Saul of Tarsus, from the region of Cicily, who engineered the charges brought against Stephen.

7.2-50 And he said, Men, brethren, and fathers, hearken; The God of glory appeared unto our father Abraham, when he was in Mesopotamia, before he dwelt in Charran,

3 And said unto him, Get thee out of thy country, and from thy kindred, and come into the land which I shall shew thee. 4 Then came he out of the land of the Chaldaeans, and dwelt in Charran: and from thence, when his father was dead, he removed him into this land, wherein ye now dwell. 5 And he gave him none inheritance in it, no, not so much as to set his foot on: yet he promised that he would give it to him for a possession, and to his seed after him, when as yet he had no child. 6 And God spake on this wise, That his seed should sojourn in a strange land; and that they should bring them into bondage, and entreat them evil four hundred years. 7 And the nation to whom they shall be in bondage will I judge, said God: and after that shall they come forth, and serve me in this place. 8 And he gave him the covenant of circumcision: and so Abraham begat Isaac, and circumcised him the eighth day; and Isaac begat Jacob; and Jacob begat the twelve patriarchs. 9 And the patriarchs, moved with envy, sold Joseph into Egypt: but God was with him, 10 And delivered him out of all his afflictions, and gave him favour and wisdom in the sight of Pharaoh king of Egypt; and he made him governor over Egypt and all his house. 11 Now there came a dearth over all the land of Egypt and Chanaan, and great affliction: and our fathers found no sustenance.12 But when Jacob heard that there was corn in Egypt, he sent out our fathers first. 13 And at the second time Joseph was made known to his brethren; and Joseph's kindred was made known unto Pharaoh. 14 Then sent Joseph,

and called his father Jacob to him, and all his kindred, threescore and fifteen souls. 15 So Jacob went down into Egypt, and died, he, and our fathers, 16 And were carried over into Sychem, and laid in the sepulchre that Abraham bought for a sum of money of the sons of Emmor the father of Sychem. 17 But when the time of the promise drew nigh, which God had sworn to Abraham, the people grew and multiplied in Egypt, 18 Till another king arose, which knew not Joseph. 19 The same dealt subtilly with our kindred, and evil entreated our fathers, so that they cast out their young children, to the end they might not live. 20 In which time Moses was born, and was exceeding fair, and nourished up in his father's house three months: 21 And when he was cast out, Pharaoh's daughter took him up, and nourished him for her own son. 22 And Moses was learned in all the wisdom of the Egyptians, and was mighty in words and in deeds. 23 And when he was full forty years old, it came into his heart to visit his brethren the children of Israel. 24 And seeing one of them suffer wrong, he defended him, and avenged him that was oppressed, and smote the Egyptian: 25 For he supposed his brethren would have understood how that God by his hand would deliver them: but they understood not. 26 And the next day he shewed himself unto them as they strove, and would have set them at one again, saying, Sirs, ye are brethren; why do ye wrong one to another? 27 But he that did his neighbour wrong thrust him away, saying, Who made thee a ruler and a judge over us? 28 Wilt thou kill me, as thou diddest the Egyptian yesterday? 29 Then fled Moses at this saying, and was a stranger in the land of Madian, where he begat two sons. 30 And when forty years were expired, there appeared to him in the wilderness of mount Sina an angel of the Lord in a flame of fire in a bush. 31 When Moses saw it, he wondered at the sight: and as he drew near to behold it, the voice of the Lord came unto him, 32 Saying, I am the God of thy fathers, the God of Abraham, and the God of Isaac, and the God of Jacob. Then Moses trembled, and durst not behold. 33 Then said the Lord to him, Put off thy shoes from thy feet: for the place where thou standest is holy ground. 34 I have seen, I have seen the affliction of my people which is in Egypt, and I have heard their groaning, and am come down to deliver them. And now come, I will send thee into Egypt. 35 This Moses whom they refused, saying, Who made thee a ruler and a judge? the same did God send to be a ruler and a deliverer by the hand of the angel which appeared to him in the bush. 36 He brought them out, after that he had shewed wonders and signs in the land of Egypt, and in the Red sea, and in the wilderness forty years. 37 This is that Moses, which said unto the children of Israel, A prophet shall the Lord your God raise up unto you of your brethren, like unto me; him shall ye hear. 38 This is he, that was in the church in the wilderness with the angel which spake to him in the mount Sina, and with our fathers: who received the lively oracles to give unto us: 39 To whom our fathers would not obey, but thrust him from them, and in their hearts turned back again into Egypt, 40 Saying unto Aaron, Make us gods to go before us: for as for this Moses, which brought us out of the land of Egypt, we wot not what is become of him. 41 And they made a calf in those days, and offered sacrifice unto the idol, and rejoiced in the works of their own hands. 42 Then God turned, and gave them up to worship the host of heaven; as it is written in the book of the prophets, O ye house of Israel, have ye offered to me slain beasts and sacrifices by the space of forty years in the wilderness? 43 Yea, ye took up the tabernacle of Moloch, and the star of your god Remphan, figures which ye made to worship them: and I will carry you away beyond Babylon. 44 Our fathers had the tabernacle of witness in the wilderness, as he had appointed, speaking unto Moses, that he should make it according to the fashion that he had seen. 45 Which also our fathers that came after brought in with Jesus into the possession of the Gentiles, whom God drave out before the face of our fathers, unto the days of David; 46 Who found favour before God, and desired to find a tabernacle for the God of Jacob. 47 But Solomon built him an house. 48 Howbeit the most High dwelleth not in temples made with hands; as saith the prophet, 49 Heaven is my throne, and earth is my footstool: what house will ye build me? saith the Lord: or what is the place of my rest? 50 Hath not my hand made all these things?

7.2-50 The book of Acts is structured around three men: Simon Peter (chapters 1-12), Saul of Tarsus chapters 13-28), and these two men are connected by Stephen. Stephen is the bridge that connects the apostle to the Jews and the apostle to the Gentiles. The immortal speech recorded here in chapter seven is possibly remembered by the brilliant Saul and later repeated to Luke for the writing of this book.

Stephen's defense~His defense begins and ends with the glory of God. Stephen presents the deliverer from bondage, Moses. He then presents their disobedience in the wilderness.

7.51-53 Ye stiffnecked and uncircumcised in heart and ears, ye do always resist the Holy Ghost: as your

fathers did, so do ye. 52 Which of the prophets have not your fathers persecuted? and they have slain them which shewed before of the coming of the Just One; of whom ye have been now the betrayers and murderers: 53 Who have received the law by the disposition of angels, and have not kept it.

7.51-53 Ye stiff-necked - This verse has no immediate connection with what precedes, and appears to have been spoken in the midst of opposition. It would seem that the Sanhedrin saw the drift of his argument, so they interrupted him. When the tumult had quieted, he addressed them in the language of this verse. He wanted to show them that they showed a character precisely similar to their rebellious fathers. The word "stiff-necked" is often used in the Old Testament, Ex 32:9; Ex 33:3; Ex 33:5; Ex 34:9; De 9:6; De 9:13; and De 10:16. It is a figurative expression taken from oxen that are hard to manage, and that will not submit to be yoked. Applied to people, it means that they are stubborn, and unwilling to submit.

7.54-60 When they heard these things, they were cut to the heart, and they gnashed on him with their teeth. 55 But he, being full of the Holy Ghost, looked up stedfastly into heaven, and saw the glory of God, and Jesus standing on the right hand of God, 56 And said, Behold, I see the heavens opened, and the Son of man standing on the right hand of God. 57 Then they cried out with a loud voice, and stopped their ears, and ran upon him with one accord, 58 And cast him out of the city, and stoned him: and the witnesses laid down their clothes at a young man's feet, whose name was Saul. 59 And they stoned Stephen, calling upon God, and saying, Lord Jesus, receive my spirit. 60 And

he kneeled down, and cried with a loud voice, Lord, lay not this sin to their charge. And when he had said this, he fell asleep.

7.54-60 These men became enraged and literally attack Stephen. They could not bear his words of truth. Many times Truth evokes this response from rebellious people. The sword of the Spirit was sharper than any two edged sword and it pierced down to the discerning of their hearts. It is a mirror God uses to see what is in the heart of a man. We all do well to measure our response to truth. Do we get angry or do we say amen? Being denied righteous justice in the tribunal of the Sanhedrin, Stephen appeals to the higher court of heaven. There Stephen finds righteous approval. When people threaten our lives because of the Gospel, we should fix our eyes on the heavenly world. God opened the curtain into another world and dimension and allowed Stephen to see the reward of those who give their life for the Gospel. It is an interesting note that the first martyr of the church was a Gentile. This is the only time that our Lord is by human lips called THE SON OF MAN after His ascension. And why here? Stephen, full of the Holy Ghost, speaking now not of himself at all (Act 7:55), but entirely by the Spirit, is led to repeat the very words in which Jesus Himself, before this same council, had foretold His glorification (Mat 26:64). It is with the blood of the first Gentile and Christian martyr still fresh that the conversion of the Gentiles begins in Chapter 8 with the Ethiopian Eunuch.

Acts 12

12.1 Now about that time Herod the king stretched forth his hands to vex certain of the church.

12.1 Herod ~ This was Herod Agrippa. He was a grandson of Herod the Great, and one of the sons of Aristobulus, as well as the brother of the infamous Herodius. Herod had put his father to death (Josephus, Antiq., 18, 5). Herod the Great left three sons, between whom his kingdom was divided - Archelaus, Philip, and Antipas. To Philip was left Iturea and Trachonitis. See Luke 3:1. To Antipas, Galilee and Perea; and to Archclaus, Judea, Idumea, and Samaria. Archclaus, being accused of cruelty, was banished by Augustus to Vienna in Gaul, and Judea was reduced to a province, and united with Syria. When Philip died, this region was granted by the Emperor Caligula to Herod Agrippa. Herod Antipas was driven, as an exile also, into Gaul, and then into Spain, and Herod Agrippa received also his tetrarchy. In the reign of Claudius also, the dominions of Herod Agrippa were still further enlarged. When Caligula was slain, Agrippa was at Rome, and having ingratiated himself into the favor of Claudius, he conferred on him also Judea and Samaria, so that his dominions were equal in extent to those of his grandfather, Herod the Great.

12.2 And he killed James the brother of John with the sword.

12.2 James, the brother of John - This was the son of Zebedee, Mat 4:21. He is commonly called James the Greater, in contrast to James, the son of Alpheus, who is called James the Less, Mat 10:3. The prediction of Jesus respecting him was thus fulfilled, Mat 20:23, "Ye shall indeed drink of my cup, and be baptized with the baptism that I am baptized with." Herod killed James with the sword; this is not the ordinary manner of the Jews.

12.3-5 And because he saw it pleased the Jews, he proceeded further to take Peter also. (Then were the days of unleavened bread.) 4 And when he had apprehended him, he put him in prison, and delivered him to four quaternions of soldiers to keep him; intending after Easter to bring him forth to the people. 5 Peter therefore was kept in prison: but prayer was made without ceasing of the church unto God for him.

12.3-5 *And because he saw that it pleased the Jews* - This was the principle on which he acted. It was not from a sense of right. It was not to do justice, and to protect the innocent. It was not to discharge the duties of a magistrate and a king, but it was to promote his own popularity. It is probable that Agrippa would have acted in this way in any circumstances. He was ambitious, vain, and fawning. He sought, as his great principle, popularity, and he was willing to sacrifice truth and justice to obtain this end. But there was also a particular reason for this in his case. He held his appointment under the Roman emperor. This foreign rule was always unpopular among the Jews. In order, therefore, to secure a peaceful reign, and to prevent insurrection and tumult, it was necessary for him to court their favor. He chose to indulge their wishes, and to fall in with their prejudices.

He took Peter ~ This was an obvious choice in that Peter was the established leader of the new group of followers of Jesus. Herod placed Peter in prison to remove him from the festivities of the Passover. Herod's intention was to remove the leadership of Christ's followers during this critical time. However, Jesus Christ had other ideas. The total number of soldiers that guarded Peter was sixteen, but a praying church is stronger than Roman soldiers. This is most likely the prison Peter had been put in back in chapter 5.

12.6-10 And when Herod would have brought him forth, the same night Peter was sleeping between two soldiers, bound with two chains: and the keepers before the door kept the prison.

7 And, behold, the angel of the Lord came upon him, and a light shined in the prison: and he smote Peter on the side, and raised him up, saying, Arise up quickly. And his chains fell off from his hands. 8 And the angel said unto him, Gird thyself, and bind on thy sandals. And so he did. And he saith unto him, Cast thy garment about thee, and follow me. 9 And he went out, and followed him; and wist not that it was true which was done by the angel; but thought he saw a vision. 10 When they were past the first and the second ward, they came unto the iron

gate that leadeth unto the city; which opened to them of his own accord: and they went out, and passed on through one street; and forthwith the angel departed from him.

12.6-10 The angelic interlude; who is the real King here, Herod? Jesus sends His ambassador (the Angel), to deliver His apostle. Right under the nose of sleeping guards and rattling chains, Peter leaves the jail unharmed. It was so supernatural even Peter himself did not fully realize what was happening until he was outside in the night air.

12.11-17 And when Peter was come to himself, he said, Now I know of a surety, that the Lord hath sent his angel, and hath delivered me out of the hand of Herod, and from all the expectation of the people of the Jews. 12 And when he had considered the thing, he came to the house of Mary the mother of John, whose surname was Mark; where many were gathered together praying. 13 And as Peter knocked at the door of the gate, a damsel came to hearken, named Rhoda. 14 And when she knew Peter's voice, she opened not the gate for gladness, but ran in, and told how Peter stood before the gate. 15 And they said unto her, Thou art mad. But she constantly affirmed that it was even so. Then said they, It is his angel. 16 But Peter continued knocking: and when they had opened the door, and saw him, they were astonished. 17 But he, beckoning unto them with the hand to hold their peace, declared unto them how the Lord had brought him out of the prison. And he said, Go shew these things unto James, and to the brethren. And he departed, and went into another place.

12.11-17 The impact of the miracle. Peter is stunned, then Rhoda is stunned, finally the church is stunned. Lastly, King Herod is stunned, as his prisoner has walked out of the prison unharmed.

12.18-25 Now as soon as it was day, there was no small stir among the soldiers, what was become of Peter. 19 And when Herod had sought for him, and found him not, he examined the keepers, and commanded that they should be put to death. And he went down from Judaea to Caesarea, and there abode. 20 And Herod was highly displeased with them of Tyre and Sidon: but they came with one accord to him, and, having made Blastus the king's chamberlain their friend, desired peace; because their country was nourished by the king's country. 21 And upon a set day Herod, arrayed in royal apparel, sat upon his throne, and made an oration unto them. 22 And the people gave a shout, saying, It is the voice of a god, and not of a man. 23 And immediately the angel of the Lord smote him, because he gave not God the glory: and he was eaten of worms, and gave up the ghost.

24 But the word of God grew and multiplied. 25 And Barnabas and Saul returned from Jerusalem, when they had fulfilled their ministry, and took with them John, whose surname was Mark.

12.18-25 Herod was the laughing stock of the entire city. Even those who hated the new Christian sect must have laughed when told of Peter's deliverance. Herod looked like the charlatan he was and Jesus looked like the Lord He is. Viola'; from the midst of sixteen soldiers the leader of the new Christian band had simply walked away from the prison. To show his paltry power Herod puts the soldiers to death and retreats beyond the raucous laughter and embarrassment. Herod slinks down to Caesarea to lick his wounds. It is there Jesus Christ finally puts the period to the long sentence concerning the Herod family. This tyrannical family had tormented the home land of God's people now for decades. While being proclaimed a god by mortals, God himself declared Herod an imposter to the throne of Israel. An angel is dispatched to end the long reign of this miserable family. The sacred writer then pens one of the most profound comparisons in the Bible. Herod is smitten and dies an ignominious death, while the word of God lives and grows.

Chapter 13

13.1-2 Now there were in the church that was at Antioch certain prophets and teachers; as Barnabas, and Simeon that was called Niger, and Lucius of Cyrene, and Manaen, which had been brought up with Herod the tetrarch, and Saul. 2 As they ministered to the Lord, and fasted, the Holy Ghost said, Separate me Barnabas and Saul for the work whereunto I have called them.

13.1-2 The hinge of Acts...Here the writer turns from the life of Peter and begins the life of Paul. The first 12 chapters were about Peter and the Jerusalem church, now the remaining chapters will be about Paul and the Gentile church. This moment is inescapable. This not the choice of Luke, but rather the choice of the Holy Ghost. This is a sovereign moment in world history. From the beginning of time God had waited patiently for this moment. His intent was to save fallen humanity, not just Israel. From a Gentile city, the new center of the Christian sect, the Holy Ghost steps in and gives sovereign direction. So they being sent forth by the Holy Ghost...Luke insures the directive is authenticated.

13.3-5 And when they had fasted and prayed, and laid their hands on them, they sent them away.

4 So they, being sent forth by the Holy Ghost, departed unto Seleucia; and from thence they sailed to Cyprus. 5 And when they were at Salamis, they preached the word of God in the synagogues of the Jews: and they had also John to their minister.

13.3-5 Barnabas and Saul set sail for Cyprus. It is on this island that momentous events occur. When they leave this island Saul will forever be known as Paul. It is here; with his first Gentile convert he jettisons his Hebrew name forever. The die is cast, his choice is made. The second thing we notice is that the roles become reversed. Barnabas has been the leader, the mentor. Now Paul takes the lead and begins his life calling.

13.6-12 And when they had gone through the isle unto Paphos, they found a certain sorcerer, a false prophet, a Jew, whose name was Barjesus: 7 Which was with the deputy of the country, Sergius Paulus, a prudent man; who called for Barnabas and Saul, and desired to hear the word of God. 8 But Elymas the sorcerer (for so is his name by interpretation) withstood them, seeking to turn away the deputy from the faith. 9 Then Saul, (who also is called Paul,) filled with the Holy Ghost, set his eyes on him. 10 And said, O full of all subtilty and all mischief, thou child of the devil, thou enemy of all righteousness, wilt thou not cease to pervert the right ways of the Lord? 11 And now, behold, the hand of the Lord is upon thee, and thou shalt be blind, not seeing the sun for a season. And immediately there fell on him a mist and a darkness; and he went about seeking some to lead him by the hand. 12 Then the

deputy, when he saw what was done, believed, being astonished at the doctrine of the Lord.

13.6-12 These few verses reveal the shift in leadership of the missionary team. Paul has become the Apostle to the Gentiles and he steps forward as the Holy Ghost places the mantle of divine authority around his shoulders. Using his Apostolic authority to smite Elymas with blindness, he asserts the prominence that will be his calling card for the next ten years throughout Asia, Acacia, Galatia, and Macedonia. Ultimately Paul would change our world forever, and this is the moment he graduates to the esteemed position of the Apostle to the Gentiles.

13.13-41 Now when Paul and his company loosed from Paphos, they came to Perga in Pamphylia: and John departing from them returned to Jerusalem. 14 But when they departed from Perga, they came to Antioch in Pisidia, and went into the synagogue on the sabbath day, and sat down. 15 And after the reading of the law and the prophets the rulers of the synagogue sent unto them, saying, Ye men and brethren, if ye have any word of exhortation for the people, say on. 16 Then Paul stood up, and beckoning with his hand said, Men of Israel, and ye that fear God, give audience. 17 The God of this people of Israel chose our fathers, and exalted the people when they dwelt as strangers in the land of Egypt, and with an high arm brought he them out of it. 18 And about the time of forty years suffered he their manners in the wilderness. 19 And when he had destroyed seven nations in the land of Chanaan, he divided their land to them by lot. 20 And after that he gave unto them judges about the space of four hundred and fifty years, until Samuel the

prophet. 21 And afterward they desired a king: and God gave unto them Saul the son of Cis, a man of the tribe of Benjamin, by the space of forty years. 22 And when he had removed him, he raised up unto them David to be their king; to whom also he gave their testimony, and said, I have found David the son of Jesse, a man after mine own heart, which shall fulfil all my will. 23 Of this man's seed hath God according to his promise raised unto Israel a Saviour, Jesus: 24 When John had first preached before his coming the baptism of repentance to all the people of Israel. 25 And as John fulfilled his course, he said, Whom think ye that I am? I am not he. But, behold, there cometh one after me, whose shoes of his feet I am not worthy to loose. 26 Men and brethren, children of the stock of Abraham, and whosoever among you feareth God, to you is the word of this salvation sent. 27 For they that dwell at Jerusalem, and their rulers, because they knew him not, nor yet the voices of the prophets which are read every sabbath day, they have fulfilled them in condemning him. 28 And though they found no cause of death in him, yet desired they Pilate that he should be slain. 29 And when they had fulfilled all that was written of him, they took him down from the tree, and laid him in a sepulchre.

30 But God raised him from the dead: 31 And he was seen many days of them which came up with him from Galilee to Jerusalem, who are his witnesses unto the people. 32 And we declare unto you glad tidings, how that the promise which was made unto the fathers, 33 God hath fulfilled the same unto us their children, in that he hath raised up Jesus again; as it is also written in the second psalm, Thou art my Son, this day have I begotten thee. 34 And as

concerning that he raised him up from the dead, now no more to return to corruption, he said on this wise, I will give you the sure mercies of David. 35 Wherefore he saith also in another psalm, Thou shalt not suffer thine Holy One to see corruption. 36 For David, after he had served his own generation by the will of God, fell on sleep, and was laid unto his fathers, and saw corruption: 37 But he, whom God raised again, saw no corruption. 38 Be it known unto you therefore, men and brethren, that through this man is preached unto you the forgiveness of sins: 39 And by him all that believe are justified from all things, from which ye could not be justified by the law of Moses. 40 Beware therefore, lest that come upon you, which is spoken of in the prophets; 41 Behold, ye despisers, and wonder, and perish: for I work a work in your days, a work which ye shall in no wise believe, though a man declare it unto you.

13.13-41 Leaving the island of Cyprus, Paul, Barnabas and John Mark return to the mainland to continue their missions work. Here an important event occurs. John Mark leaves and returns to Jerusalem. This would later cause a rift between Paul and Barnabas at the beginning of the second missionary journey. Paul would choose Silas to accompany him and Barnabas fades from the script. Paul and Barnabas go to the synagogue at Antioch and continue their mission. Paul affirms that Jesus is the Messiah and God manifest in the flesh (1 Tim 3.16). He proves this by the fulfillment of the scriptures using the Judges, David and the Psalms.

13.42-52 And when the Jews were gone out of the synagogue, the Gentiles besought that these words

might be preached to them the next sabbath. **43** Now when the congregation was broken up, many of the Jews and religious proselytes followed Paul and Barnabas: who, speaking to them, persuaded them to continue in the grace of God. **44** And the next sabbath day came almost the whole city together to hear the word of God. **45** But when the Jews saw the multitudes, they were filled with envy, and spake against those things which were spoken by Paul, contradicting and blaspheming. **46** Then Paul and Barnabas waxed bold, and said, It was necessary that the word of God should first have been spoken to you: but seeing ye put it from you, and judge yourselves unworthy of everlasting life, lo, we turn to the Gentiles. **47** For so hath the Lord commanded us, saying, I have set thee to be a light of the Gentiles, that thou shouldest be for salvation unto the ends of the earth. **48** And when the Gentiles heard this, they were glad, and glorified the word of the Lord: and as many as were ordained to eternal life believed. **49** And the word of the Lord was published throughout all the region. **50** But the Jews stirred up the devout and honourable women, and the chief men of the city, and raised persecution against Paul and Barnabas, and expelled them out of their coasts. **51** But they shook off the dust of their feet against them, and came unto Iconium. **52** And the disciples were filled with joy, and with the Holy Ghost.

13.42-52 Here is another defining moment in the worldwide spread of the Gospel of Jesus Christ. Paul presents it to Jew and Gentile alike. All who accept it are received into the church. Those who reject it are no longer under the covenant. Those who reject truth so often then turn to persecuting the truth. These Jewish rejecters seek notable women and leaders of the city to persecute Paul and Barnabas. The word of God was published throughout the whole region, and the disciples had great joy.

Chapter 14

14.1-7 And it came to pass in Iconium, that they went both together into the synagogue of the Jews, and so spake, that a great multitude both of the Jews and also of the Greeks believed. 2 But the unbelieving Jews stirred up the Gentiles, and made their minds evil affected against the brethren.

3 Long time therefore abode they speaking boldly in the Lord, which gave testimony unto the word of his grace, and granted signs and wonders to be done by their hands. 4 But the multitude of the city was divided: and part held with the Jews, and part with the apostles. 5 And when there was an assault made both of the Gentiles, and also of the Jews with their rulers, to use them despitefully, and to stone them, 6 They were ware of it, and fled unto Lystra and Derbe, cities of Lycaonia, and unto the region that lieth round about: 7 And there they preached the gospel.

14.1-7 Iconium...this city shows a bi-polar reaction to Paul's preaching from the people. Success and opposition both surface at Iconium. Iconium was a considerable city of Asia Minor. From Pliny's description it would appear to have been a populous and important city at the time of Paul's visit. Under the Byzantine emperors it was the metropolis of Lycaonia. The Apostles immediately begin their work. Persecution made them change their place, but not their purpose. Neither did they abandon their method of working. Though they had turned to the Gentiles, they had not turned away from the Jews. The now developing pattern continued; the Jews were the most bitter enemies to the preaching. The Apostles spoke boldly. The threatening cloud of danger did not diminish their courage. The preaching caused a divide. True preaching is confrontational and causes people to make choices. Being persecuted in this city, they followed Jesus' injunction, and moved on to the next city. "And there they preached the gospel." Persecution pushed the gospel to new places. Paul's preaching at Iconium was like Themistocles, the Athenian general, urging a point in a council of war. Theristocles provoked the displeasure of Eurybiades, the Spartan, who was the commander-in-chief. Eurybiades lifted up his cane over his head in a menacing posture to strike Theristocles. Strike said Theristocles, but hear me. Eurybiades did hear him, and the country was saved. So Paul having heard of impending danger, saved some souls and moved on to Lystra.

14.8-18 And there sat a certain man at Lystra, impotent in his feet, being a cripple from his mother's womb, who never had walked: 9 The same heard Paul speak: who stedfastly beholding him, and perceiving that he had faith to be healed, 10 Said with a loud voice, Stand upright on thy feet. And he leaped and walked. 11 And when the people saw what Paul had

done, they lifted up their voices, saying in the speech of Lycaonia, The gods are come down to us in the likeness of men.

12 And they called Barnabas, Jupiter; and Paul, Mercurius, because he was the chief speaker. 13 Then the priest of Jupiter, which was before their city, brought oxen and garlands unto the gates, and would have done sacrifice with the people. 14 Which when the apostles, Barnabas and Paul, heard of, they rent their clothes, and ran in among the people, crying out, 15 And saying, Sirs, why do ye these things? We also are men of like passions with you, and preach unto you that ye should turn from these vanities unto the living God, which made heaven, and earth, and the sea, and all things that are therein: 16 Who in times past suffered all nations to walk in their own ways.

17 Nevertheless he left not himself without witness, in that he did good, and gave us rain from heaven, and fruitful seasons, filling our hearts with food and gladness. 18 And with these sayings scarce restrained they the people, that they had not done sacrifice unto them.

14.8-18 Lystra was situated in the highlands, amid a wild, mountainous country and was in a different province. It had been made a province by Augustus. It was such a dry area water was actually sold there. Paul began preaching there, and an impotent man who had never walked was listening and watching. Paul speaks to him and the man who had never walked leaps to his feet and walks. This mighty miracle galvanizes the populace. They react the only way they know how; they turn to their historical gods. They announce the gods have come down in the form of man. Paul and Barnabas immediately use this incident to preach Jesus unto the people.

14.19-23 And there came thither certain Jews from Antioch and Iconium, who persuaded the people, and having stoned Paul, drew him out of the city, supposing he had been dead. 20 Howbeit, as the disciples stood round about him, he rose up, and came into the city: and the next day he departed with Barnabas to Derbe. 21 And when they had preached the gospel to that city, and had taught many, they returned again to Lystra, and to Iconium, and Antioch, 22 Confirming the souls of the disciples, and exhorting them to continue in the faith, and that we must through much tribulation enter into the kingdom of God. 23 And when they had ordained them elders in every church, and had prayed with fasting, they commended them to the Lord, on whom they believed.

14.19-23 The Jews that hated Paul came from Antioch and Iconium and spread their lies and hatred until it ran cold and hard through the veins of the very people who had proclaimed Paul and Barnabas gods. The inflamed crowd stones Paul and thinking him dead, drag him out of the city, and leave him there, not even providing a burial. The disciples watch amazed as Paul rises as though from the dead and goes to Derbe. Showing no fear, when Paul makes his return trip he goes right back to the place of his stoning. Paul comforts the saints in the cities where churches were begun, and begins the return journey to the church at Antioch.

14.24-28 And after they had passed throughout Pisidia, they came to Pamphylia. 25 And when they had preached the word in Perga, they went down into Attalia: 26 And thence sailed to Antioch, from whence they had been recommended to the grace of God for the work which they fulfilled. 27 And when they were come, and had gathered the church together, they rehearsed all that God had done with them, and how he had opened the door of faith unto the Gentiles. 28 And there they abode long time with the disciples.

14.24-28 The first missionary journey to the Gentile world comes to a conclusion. Peter had gone to the house of Cornelius, and Philip had gone to Gaza, but this was purely a missions endeavor to Gentile lands. It would be eclipsed by a second and third journey, but nonetheless it was an amazing success. There was much rejoicing in the Antioch church when the report was given. The gospel of Jesus Christ had a beachhead and it would revolutionize the known world in the next three hundred years. Planet earth would never be the same. The door had opened (1 Cor 16.9, 2 Cor 2.12, Col 4.3) and Paul boldly walked through the door to forever change our world.

Chapter 15

15.1 And certain men which came down from Judaea taught the brethren, and said, Except ye be circumcised after the manner of Moses, ye cannot be saved.

15.1 In all the Bible there are just a few real watershed moments. Acts 15 is one of those moments. The single most important change in the new church occurs at this council. The division among leaders is intense and they need a solution. The meeting is confrontational. Circumcision was the leading or principal rite of the Jewish religion. It was indispensable to the name and privileges of a Jew. Proselytes to their religion were circumcised as well as native-born Jews, and they held it to be indispensable to salvation. It is evident from this that Paul and Barnabas had dispensed with this rite in regard to the Gentile converts, and that they intended to found the Christian church on the principle that the Jewish ceremonies were to cease.

15.2-11 When therefore Paul and Barnabas had no small dissension and disputation with them, they determined that Paul and Barnabas, and certain other of them, should go up to Jerusalem unto the apostles and elders about this question. 3 And being brought

on their way by the church, they passed through Phenice and Samaria, declaring the conversion of the Gentiles: and they caused great joy unto all the brethren. 4 And when they were come to Jerusalem, they were received of the church, and of the apostles and elders, and they declared all things that God had done with them. 5 But there rose up certain of the sect of the Pharisees which believed, saying, That it was needful to circumcise them, and to command them to keep the law of Moses. 6 And the apostles and elders came together for to consider of this matter. 7 And when there had been much disputing, Peter rose up, and said unto them, Men and brethren, ye know how that a good while ago God made choice among us, that the Gentiles by my mouth should hear the word of the gospel, and believe. 8 And God, which knoweth the hearts, bare them witness, giving them the Holy Ghost, even as he did unto us; 9 And put no difference between us and them, purifying their hearts by faith. 10 Now therefore why tempt ye God, to put a yoke upon the neck of the disciples, which neither our fathers nor we were able to bear? 11 But we believe that through the grace of the Lord Jesus Christ we shall be saved, even as they.

15.2-11 Dissension here is the Greek word stasis, and denotes intestine war. We would use a modern term "gut wrenching". Important principles were to be settled in regard to the organization of the church. Much was at stake in the decision of this gathering of the Church. If the Jewish party triumphed, Christianity sank to the level of a Jewish sect. The proponents of following Moses raised the question of circumcision. They contended that the way from Paganism to Christ must be through Moses. They especially insisted that Gentiles must become Jews by submitting to the initial rite of circumcision. This oppositional teaching followed Paul throughout his life, and produced many of the noble arguments and appeals of his epistles. We can easily understand the vehemence with which he protested. Finally it was determined to submit the question to the judgment of the Apostles and elders in Jerusalem. The journey to Jerusalem was a triumphal progress. The story of the Gentile conversions that God had produced with the labors of the two missionaries, not only filled all hearts with joy, but was the conclusive answer to the Judaizing teachers who were the cause of all the trouble. The question as to the conditions on which Gentiles could be received into Christian communion had already been raised by the case of Cornelius, but it became more acute after Paul's missionary journey. The struggle between the narrower and broader views was bound to come to a head. The first address at the meeting was by Peter, who quoted his own experience at the household of Cornelius. He contended that God accepted the Gentiles (without circumcision), the same as He accepted the Jews (with circumcision). This is the last time we hear of Simon Peter in Acts.

15.12 Then all the multitude kept silence, and gave audience to Barnabas and Paul, declaring what miracles and wonders God had wrought among the Gentiles by them.

15.12 Next came the reports from Paul and Barnabas about the many conversions of Gentiles.

15.13-21 And after they had held their peace, James answered, saying, Men and brethren, hearken unto me: 14 Simeon hath declared how God at the first did

visit the Gentiles, to take out of them a people for his name. 15 And to this agree the words of the prophets; as it is written, 16 After this I will return, and will build again the tabernacle of David, which is fallen down; and I will build again the ruins thereof, and I will set it up: 17 That the residue of men might seek after the Lord, and all the Gentiles, upon whom my name is called, saith the Lord, who doeth all these things.

18 Known unto God are all his works from the beginning of the world. 19 Wherefore my sentence is, that we trouble not them, which from among the Gentiles are turned to God: 20 But that we write unto them, that they abstain from pollutions of idols, and from fornication, and from things strangled, and from blood. 21 For Moses of old time hath in every city them that preach him, being read in the synagogues every Sabbath day.

15.13-21 James, the leader of the church in Jerusalem, spoke next. James had a prominent position in the Jerusalem church, because he was the Lord's brother and a man of remarkable holiness and prayerfulness. He laid emphasis on the divine program, which moved forward from Jew to Gentile, from the rebuilding of the ruined Tabernacle of David to the seeking of the Lord by the residue of men. The implication was that though God dwelt in a special manner with the Jewish people, the Gentiles would come seeking Him directly and without becoming incorporated with the Jews.

15.22-35 Then pleased it the apostles and elders with the whole church, to send chosen men of their own company to Antioch with Paul and Barnabas;

namely, Judas surnamed Barsabas and Silas, chief men among the brethren: 23 And they wrote letters by them after this manner; The apostles and elders and brethren send greeting unto the brethren which are of the Gentiles in Antioch and Syria and Cilicia. 24 Forasmuch as we have heard, that certain which went out from us have troubled you with words, subverting your souls, saying, Ye must be circumcised, and keep the law: to whom we gave no such commandment: 25 It seemed good unto us, being assembled with one accord, to send chosen men unto you with our beloved Barnabas and Paul, 26 Men that have hazarded their lives for the name of our Lord Jesus Christ. 27 We have sent therefore Judas and Silas, who shall also tell you the same things by mouth. 28 For it seemed good to the Holy Ghost, and to us, to lay upon you no greater burden than these necessary things; 29 That ye abstain from meats offered to idols, and from blood, and from things strangled, and from fornication: from which if ye keep yourselves, ye shall do well. Fare ye well. 30 So when they were dismissed, they came to Antioch: and when they had gathered the multitude together, they delivered the epistle:

31 Which when they had read, they rejoiced for the consolation. 32 And Judas and Silas, being prophets also themselves, exhorted the brethren with many words, and confirmed them. 33 And after they had tarried there a space, they were let go in peace from the brethren unto the apostles.

34 Notwithstanding it pleased Silas to abide there still. 35 Paul also and Barnabas continued in Antioch, teaching and preaching the word of the Lord, with many others also.

15.22-35 The letter: What letter in the history of the world is signally as important as this letter? This one hand written document affects the future of planet earth and all of eternity. By this one decree, untold millions will be freed from the bond of Jewish religion. The multitudes of Asia, Acacia, Macedonia and Galatia, are seen as equals in Christ Jesus. What a monumental moment. The wall that had been between the Jew and the Gentile was finally broken down. It was solved in the Holy Ghost. The manifold rejoicing that must have swept through the Gentile converts. That letter still affects us to this day. We have never been the same, and are forever changed. Upon the return to Antioch, the epistle is read. There was great rejoicing, spiritual harmony, and peace in the church.

15.36-41 And some days after Paul said unto Barnabas, Let us go again and visit our brethren in every city where we have preached the word of the Lord, and see how they do. 37 And Barnabas determined to take with them John, whose surname was Mark. 38 But Paul thought not good to take him with them, who departed from them from Pamphylia, and went not with them to the work. 39 And the contention was so sharp between them, that they departed asunder one from the other: and so Barnabas took Mark, and sailed unto Cyprus; 40 And Paul chose Silas, and departed, being recommended by the brethren unto the grace of God. 41 And he went through Syria and Cilicia, confirming the churches.

15.36-41 The Bible does not hide our moments of human element. Paul and Barnabas had just witnessed the greatest decision made in the New Testament. They had witnessed first hand the healing hand of the Holy

Ghost direct the church for worldwide evangelism. In the next verse, these two men could not resolve a simple disagreement of who should accompany them on the visit to the churches they had established. The disagreement became so intense, they parted ways. Barnabas goes home (Cyprus), and fades from Bible history forever. Paul embarks on missionary journey number two and continues to change the known world with the gospel of Jesus Christ. The power of a heated decision proves it can change your future forever. And Paul chose Silas, and departed, being recommended by the brethren.

Chapter 16

16.1-2 Then came he to Derbe and Lystra: and, behold, a certain disciple was there, named Timotheus, the son of a certain woman, which was a Jewess, and believed; but his father was a Greek: 2 Which was well reported of by the brethren that were at Lystra and Iconium.

16.1-2 Thus begins the second missionary journey of the Apostle Paul. One of the great things on this journey is the addition of Timothy to Paul's life. Paul will style him "his own son in the faith" 1 Ti 1.2. The great Apostle seemed to have a gift to establish and train young men as in Timothy, Titus, and even Mark. On this second journey, the gospel of Jesus Christ will be preached in Europe for the first time. The original twelve Apostles seem reticent to take the gospel to the Gentile masses. This is possibly the reason for Paul's extraordinary call to be an Apostle. Paul went far beyond any other Apostle's vision and preaching.

16.3 Him would Paul have to go forth with him; and took and circumcised him because of the Jews which were in those quarters: for they knew all that his father was a Greek.

16.3 It is interesting that Paul deferred to the Jews and had Timothy circumcised following the Jerusalem council. This is especially so because they were going to the churches to deliver the decrees that were ordained at Jerusalem and this included circumcision, which was no longer required of Gentile converts. Timothy is to become an integral part of the ministry and legacy of Paul. Paul sends him from Corinth to the Thessalonians, from Ephesus to the Corinthians, and eventually leaves Timothy to succeed him at Ephesus. More dazzling names than Timothy are to be seen in the firmament of the early Church. Apollos flames across the sky, leaving behind the brilliant sparks of his Alexandrian rhetoric, but the star of Timothy is the steady North Star of Paul's legacy.

16.4-5 And as they went through the cities, they delivered them the decrees for to keep, that were ordained of the apostles and elders which were at Jerusalem. 5 And so were the churches established in the faith, and increased in number daily.

16.4-5 Paul and Silas now visit the churches that had been established on the previous missionary journey to announce the decision of the council in Jerusalem. The churches were established and increased daily.

16.6-10 Now when they had gone throughout Phrygia and the region of Galatia, and were forbidden of the Holy Ghost to preach the word in Asia, 7 After they were come to Mysia, they assayed to go into Bithynia: but the Spirit suffered them not. 8 And they passing by Mysia came down to Troas.

9 And a vision appeared to Paul in the night;

There stood a man of Macedonia, and prayed him, saying, Come over into Macedonia, and help us. 10 And after he had seen the vision, immediately we endeavoured to go into Macedonia, assuredly gathering that the Lord had called us for to preach the gospel unto them.

16.6-10 The Holy Ghost now directs Paul to the next level of missionary expansion. It is now time to open the door to Europe with the manifesto of Jesus Christ. Troas had been his farthest travels north to date. The great Apostle sets foot on the continent of Europe. The door to Asia was closed by the Holy Ghost. They attempted to go to Bithynia, but the Spirit said no again. Jesus Christ was charting His course of the triumph of the gospel as sure as any world conqueror. While at Troas Paul has a vision. A man from Macedonia beckons him. Having received Divine direction, they embark with a straight course. The now seasoned, experienced, missionary Apostle takes on a new continent and the cities fall to the Gospel of Jesus Christ. The roll call is impressive: Philippi, Thessalonica, Berea, Athens, and finally Corinth, the sight of the world's greatest revival in history. The next three years are unequaled in missionary work in the scriptures. Paul's greatest victories and harshest defeats await him in Europe. He is ready, he begins at Philippi.

16.11-15 Therefore loosing from Troas, we came with a straight course to Samothracia, and the next day to Neapolis; 12 And from thence to Philippi, which is the chief city of that part of Macedonia, and a colony: and we were in that city abiding certain days. 13 And on the sabbath we went out of the city by a river side, where prayer was wont to be made; and we sat down,

and spake unto the women which resorted thither. **14 And a certain woman named Lydia, a seller of purple, of the city of Thyatira, which worshipped God, heard us: whose heart the Lord opened, that she attended unto the things which were spoken of Paul. 15 And when she was baptized, and her household, she besought us, saying, If ye have judged me to be faithful to the Lord, come into my house, and abide there. And she constrained us.**

16.11-15 Philippi was a city built by King Philip, Alexander the Great's father. Not long before Paul arrived it had been the scene of a great battle between Brutus and Cassius against Mark Antony and Augustus. The battle decided the fate of the Roman Empire and influenced the course of world history. Now another battle was to be fought. A spiritual battle, the beachhead of Europe. Paul is a seasoned Spiritual warrior. Five years later, when writing his second letter to the church at Corinth, he tells us he had already been shipwrecked three times. It appears there was no Synagogue in Philippi, so Paul goes to the riverside. The original name of Philippi was Crenides (Place of streams). The first message on the European continent is preached on a riverbank, with a nod to John the Baptist, the Gospel gains the first Convert: a woman. The spiritual war for Europe has begun. The battle is engaged.

16.16-24 And it came to pass, as we went to prayer, a certain damsel possessed with a spirit of divination met us, which brought her masters much gain by soothsaying: 17 The same followed Paul and us, and cried, saying, These men are the servants of the most high God, which shew unto us the way of salvation. 18 And this did she many days. But Paul, being

grieved, turned and said to the spirit, I command thee in the name of Jesus Christ to come out of her. And he came out the same hour. 19 And when her masters saw that the hope of their gains was gone, they caught Paul and Silas, and drew them into the marketplace unto the rulers, 20 And brought them to the magistrates, saying, These men, being Jews, do exceedingly trouble our city, 21 And teach customs, which are not lawful for us to receive, neither to observe, being Romans. 22 And the multitude rose up together against them: and the magistrates rent off their clothes, and commanded to beat them. 23 And when they had laid many stripes upon them, they cast them into prison, charging the jailor to keep them safely: 24 Who, having received such a charge, thrust them into the inner prison, and made their feet fast in the stocks.

16.16-24 The battle intensifies. Satan counter attacks with a demon possessed girl. Having lost a female to the gospel, Satan launches a female at the Apostles. Lydia, saved and redeemed versus a damsel full of the spirit of iniquity. The stage was the city. The population of the city was the audience. For several days it looked like a stand off. Paul was grieved (diaponeo-be worried). Paul understood the war. He speaks to the spirit rather than the damsel. Jesus Christ shows Philippi He is the ruler. The spirit leaves the girl. In frustration the devil turns the masters of the damsel against Paul. A battle won, but the war for Europe continues. Paul and Silas are beaten and jailed. This sets the stage for yet another incredible triumph of the gospel.

16.25-34 And at midnight Paul and Silas prayed, and sang praises unto God: and the prisoners heard them.

26 And suddenly there was a great earthquake, so that the foundations of the prison were shaken: and immediately all the doors were opened, and every one's bands were loosed. 27 And the keeper of the prison awaking out of his sleep, and seeing the prison doors open, he drew out his sword, and would have killed himself, supposing that the prisoners had been fled. 28 But Paul cried with a loud voice, saying, Do thyself no harm: for we are all here. 29 Then he called for a light, and sprang in, and came trembling, and fell down before Paul and Silas, 30 And brought them out, and said, Sirs, what must I do to be saved? 31 And they said, Believe on the Lord Jesus Christ, and thou shalt be saved, and thy house. 32 And they spake unto him the word of the Lord, and to all that were in his house. 33 And he took them the same hour of the night, and washed their stripes; and was baptized, he and all his, straightway. 34 And when he had brought them into his house, he set meat before them, and rejoiced, believing in God with all his house.

16.25-34 Two apostles, badly beaten, chained, and jailed, still triumph. Demons must have been baffled. What more could they do to stop these apostles? Paul and Silas at their lowest still triumphed over the demonic world. At midnight these weary soldiers of the cross begin to sing. They had been beaten with sticks (rhabdizo- to strike with a stick). They were in the deepest recess of the prison. Suddenly the other prisoners heard them singing. Then God defended his Apostles with a mighty earthquake. Every jail door is open, prisoners are loose. The jailer attempts to kill himself and Paul snatches victory and conversion of a lost soul out of the confusion. The terrified jailer asks what he must do to be saved. Paul instructs him to believe on the Lord

Jesus Christ. The jailer takes them to his home, feeds them, and his whole house is baptized. This instance shows what true believing is. When the Jailer believed he acted. James 2.6 mirrors this with the statement "faith without works is dead". True faith always brings action. To believe on the Lord Jesus Christ means to repent, be baptized and receive the Holy Ghost. This is the common salvation of the book of Acts in chapter two, chapter eight, chapter ten, and chapter nineteen.

16.35-40 And when it was day, the magistrates sent the serjeants, saying, Let those men go. 36 And the keeper of the prison told this saying to Paul, The magistrates have sent to let you go: now therefore depart, and go in peace. 37 But Paul said unto them, They have beaten us openly uncondemned, being Romans, and have cast us into prison; and now do they thrust us out privily? nay verily; but let them come themselves and fetch us out. 38 And the serjeants told these words unto the magistrates: and they feared, when they heard that they were Romans. 39 And they came and besought them, and brought them out, and desired them to depart out of the city. 40 And they went out of the prison, and entered into the house of Lydia: and when they had seen the brethren, they comforted them, and departed.

16.35-40 The rulers sent to let the Apostles go. Jesus Christ had already set them at liberty. When these rulers ask Paul to leave, Paul invokes his Roman privilege. The magistrates are made aware of their illegal conduct against Paul who was a Roman citizen. Now the battle for Europe has turned again. These Roman magistrates besought (parakaleo-to call near, invite) Paul and Silas and gently asked them to depart. Paul and Silas did not leave town as condemned men, but rather as servants of the Lord Jesus Christ. They stopped at the house of Lydia, saw the brethren, and departed like true ambassadors should. The first citadel of Europe, the church at Philippi, was safely in the hands of Jesus Christ.

Chapter 17

17.1 Now when they had passed through Amphipolis and Apollonia, they came to Thessalonica, where was a synagogue of the Jews:

17.1 The missionaries pass through Amphipolis and Apollonia and arrive in Thessalonica via the great Egnatian road. We are left to wonder why the Apostle does not stop and preach at Amphipolis, which is the capital city of this region of Macedonia. Possibly because there was no synagogue? Maybe his mantra was conquer the cities and the villages will fall of themselves? That seems to be the policy that swept through the empire like a prairie fire. It is 33 miles from Philippi to Amphipolis, another 30 miles to Apollonia and 37 more on to Thessalonica. It would seem the Apostle must have stopped for lodging in these cities, yet he does not linger to preach.

17.2-4 And Paul, as his manner was, went in unto them, and three sabbath days reasoned with them out of the scriptures, 3 Opening and alleging, that Christ must needs have suffered, and risen again from the dead; and that this Jesus, whom I preach unto you, is Christ. 4 And some of them believed, and consorted

with Paul and Silas; and of the devout Greeks a great multitude, and of the chief women not a few.

17.2-4 For three Sabbath days Paul reasons that Jesus is the Christ. Luke the writer of Acts includes the fact that chief women were a large part of the conversion of souls here in Thessalonica. One interesting note is how quickly Paul was able to begin churches. It was always a matter of weeks and a conversion occurred.

17.5-10 But the Jews which believed not, moved with envy, took unto them certain lewd fellows of the baser sort, and gathered a company, and set all the city on an uproar, and assaulted the house of Jason, and sought to bring them out to the people. 6 And when they found them not, they drew Jason and certain brethren unto the rulers of the city, crying, These that have turned the world upside down are come hither also; 7 Whom Jason hath received: and these all do contrary to the decrees of Caesar, saying that there is another king, one Jesus. 8 And they troubled the people and the rulers of the city, when they heard these things. 9 And when they had taken security of Jason, and of the other, they let them go. 10 And the brethren immediately sent away Paul and Silas by night unto Berea: who coming thither went into the synagogue of the Jews.

17.5-10 Thessalonica...the spiritual battle for Europe is rejoined on another battlefront. Again, the enemy is the Jewish sector resisting Jesus Christ as the messiah. A church is again quickly founded, and is the first of Paul's churches to receive a letter from him in the near future. (1Thessalonians). The opposition from the Jews is so intense Paul's brethren immediately send

Paul away. How long did Paul stay in Thessalonica? This account in Acts would suggest a short time. If we look at Paul's letter written a few months later to the Thessalonican church, we can get additional insight. It is evident Paul stayed long enough to convert and establish converted idolaters. We are also made aware he was in Thessalonica long enough to receive financial support two times from the church at Philippi. Paul recounts how he worked while he was there (2.9) With this insight it is probable that Paul spent a few months in Thessalonica.

17.11-15 These were more noble than those in Thessalonica, in that they received the word with all readiness of mind, and searched the scriptures daily, whether those things were so. 12 Therefore many of them believed; also of honourable women which were Greeks, and of men, not a few. 13 But when the Jews of Thessalonica had knowledge that the word of God was preached of Paul at Berea, they came thither also, and stirred up the people. 14 And then immediately the brethren sent away Paul to go as it were to the sea: but Silas and Timotheus abode there still. 15 And they that conducted Paul brought him unto Athens: and receiving a commandment unto Silas and Timotheus for to come to him with all speed, they departed.

17.11-15 Paul takes the battle to Berea. Berea is not as large as Thessalonica. The preaching of the gospel takes root once again. Many of them believed, including honorable women who were Greeks. There were also a number of men who believed. These believers in Berea were called nobel by Paul, (nobel= yoog-en'-ace= high born). This would infer a higher level of learning as a rule. The gospel need never fear education or learning.

Here the great Apostle proves that even education is no match for the gospel in the battle for Europe. However, Paul's enemies from Thessalonica arrive in Berea to continue their assault on the gospel. Like hunters seeking prey they attack Paul again. These gospel haters stir up the people, so Paul is sent away for safety. He starts as though to go by ship. Paul leaves Timothy and Silas with the new believers. Paul leaves for Athens. The world center of humanism and philosophy. It is at Athens Paul has his greatest defeat. That battle almost took down the great apostle.

17.16-19 Now while Paul waited for them at Athens, his spirit was stirred in him, when he saw the city wholly given to idolatry. 17 Therefore disputed he in the synagogue with the Jews, and with the devout persons, and in the market daily with them that met with him. 18 Then certain philosophers of the Epicureans, and of the Stoicks, encountered him. And some said, What will this babbler say? other some, He seemeth to be a setter forth of strange gods: because he preached unto them Jesus, and the resurrection. 19 And they took him, and brought him unto Areopagus, saying, May we know what this new doctrine, whereof thou speakest, is?

17.16-19 Paul feels he is ready. He has fought some battles for some cities and they have fallen to the gospel of Jesus Christ. What thoughts must have looped through the mind of the great Apostle as he saw Athens on the horizon. What dreams he must have entertained. With Philippi, Thessalonica, and Berea on his list of great victories and conquered cities, Paul enters Athens. He attends the synagogue, as is his custom. The idolatry is rampant throughout the city. Athens is a stronghold for false gods. Paul goes to the market place and daily preaches and teaches. He is noticed by the elite philosophers of the city, the Epicureans and the Stoicks. Some of them mock, but others are mildly interested. This entertaining of new ideas was the Athenian pastime. It is interesting where they bring Paul. They bring him to the Areopagus, which is ar'-i-os pa'-gos in the original. This name is the name of the Greek deity of war. If there was any doubt until now that they were in a war for Europe, that doubt is dispelled. It is the Gospel of Jesus Christ against the Greek God of War. Epicureans and Stoicks smugly square off with God's greatest mind among men. The Epicureans, believers in Hedonism and pursuing life's greatest pleasure and learning, joined the Stoicks, who believed in no outward show of emotion and remaining calm, to face off against Paul. It was a world-class battle. All of Paul's life, history, intellect and training were challenged. They asked Paul point blank, what is this new doctrine?

17.20-34 For thou bringest certain strange things to our ears: we would know therefore what these things mean. 21 (For all the Athenians and strangers which were there spent their time in nothing else, but either to tell, or to hear some new thing.) 22 Then Paul stood in the midst of Mars' hill, and said, Ye men of Athens, I perceive that in all things ye are too superstitious. 23 For as I passed by, and beheld your devotions, I found an altar with this inscription, To The Unknown God. Whom therefore ye ignorantly worship, him declare I unto you. 24 God that made the world and all things therein, seeing that he is Lord of heaven and earth, dwelleth not in temples made with hands; 25 Neither is worshipped with men's hands, as though he needed any thing, seeing he giveth to all life, and breath, and

all things; 26 And hath made of one blood all nations of men for to dwell on all the face of the earth, and hath determined the times before appointed, and the bounds of their habitation; 27 That they should seek the Lord, if haply they might feel after him, and find him, though he be not far from every one of us: 28 For in him we live, and move, and have our being; as certain also of your own poets have said, For we are also his offspring. 29 Forasmuch then as we are the offspring of God, we ought not to think that the Godhead is like unto gold, or silver, or stone, graven by art and man's device. 30 And the times of this ignorance God winked at; but now commandeth all men every where to repent: 31 Because he hath appointed a day, in the which he will judge the world in righteousness by that man whom he hath ordained; whereof he hath given assurance unto all men, in that he hath raised him from the dead. 32 And when they heard of the resurrection of the dead, some mocked: and others said, We will hear thee again of this matter.   33 So Paul departed from among them. 34 Howbeit certain men clave unto him, and believed: among the which was Dionysius the Areopagite, and a woman named Damaris, and others with them.

17.20-34 The Athenian was religious. The innumerable temples, statues, and altars prove his religion. It also reveals what his religion was. It was one, which made him a splendid animal with a splendid intellect. One, which had no power against sin and fatalism. Like the sun, while it preserves the living, it hastens the decay of the dead. Possibly it was here Paul first thought if one died for all, then were all dead. Three hundred years before, in his little garden beside the market place, Epicurus had taught his followers that happiness is the great purpose and pursuit of life. The Stoics taught a system of ethics at odds with this. While the Epicurean had made the world conform to self, the Stoic had made self conform to the world. Self-gratification became the doctrine of the one, and self-denial of the other. While the Epicurean avoided pain, the Stoic welcomed it. The Stoic found the secret of life in living in conformity to nature, receiving its bitter as sweet, and its sweet as bitter, with equal composure. These polar extremes joined in an unusual show of force to challenge the Gospel of Jesus Christ. The battle did not end there in Athens that day. It has been fought, and still is fought on innumerable battlefields all over planet earth. Athens was a microcosm of humanism versus the manifesto of Jesus Christ. The great Apostle Paul gleans one soul, Dionysius, from the opposition, and a hand full of others, but he leaves Athens on his own. No one asked Paul to leave as at the other battlefronts. Paul was discouraged. Human wisdom was a standoff with human wisdom. Somewhere between Athens and Corinth, Paul made the decision that forever changed our world. He decided he would preach nothing save Jesus Christ and him crucified. That mantra, sifted from the ashes of the battle for Europe at Athens, brought the greatest revival in the history of the world. It still brings the greatest revival.

The next stop on Paul's journey is the city of Corinth. In the Apostle's first letter to them he states the Greeks seek wisdom (1Cor1.22). God allowed Paul to see what man's wisdom can achieve in the city of Athens. Then God allowed the Apostle Paul to see what the power of God can do in contrast to man's wisdom. In Athens there were a half dozen converts. In Corinth, tens of thousands of converts.

Chapter 18

18.1-2 After these things Paul departed from Athens, and came to Corinth; 2 And found a certain Jew named Aquila, born in Pontus, lately come from Italy, with his wife Priscilla; (because that Claudius had commanded all Jews to depart from Rome:) and came unto them.

18.1-2 *After these things Paul departed from Athens, and came to Corinth*; these words are the harbinger of the greatest revival in world history. The number of converts historians give varies from a low of 40,000 to a high of 80,000 in 18 months. That is 80 weeks. If these numbers can be trusted that is between 500-1000 people average each week. Not only were there great numbers but also there were some very notable people. It is no coincidence the God of eternity sets these two cities side by side and shows the results. Athens is humanism par excellence. Corinth is the power of God at it's best. Somewhere on the road between Athens and Corinth the great Apostle Paul decided he would only preach Jesus Christ and him crucified. That would be his plan and only plan. Paul laid aside every human weapon of learning and wisdom. The first field of that mantra was Corinth and the results are unparalleled in human history. May we always remember revival is in the power of Jesus Christ.

The city of Corinth was the second largest city in the Roman Empire with a population of 700,000. It was a blue-collar town with a working population. It had been destroyed and conquered by the Romans about 100 years before so it boasted some magnificent and new architecture. Corinth was a wide-open sinful city much like Las Vegas in the United States today. There was a hodge podge of people from all over the Roman Empire. There were nobility, sailors, soldiers, and every strata of life. There was no place less likely to have a revival. The pagan temple sitting on the hill side used 1000 prostitutes to pander it's sinful idolatry. When the Apostle arrived he was a beaten man by his own testimony. He spoke of despairing of life, 2 Cor 1.8. So you have the least most likely city to have a revival in the Empire, and the great Apostle at his weakest. This formula produced the world's greatest revival of the New Testament era. The preaching of the cross and the wisdom of God produced thousands of transformed lives. It still does.

18.3 And because he was of the same craft, he abode with them, and wrought: for by their occupation they were tentmakers.

18.3 Aquilla. His name means eagle. He and his wife were forced from Rome due to the edict from Emperor Claudius. (Suetonius, the Roman historian says Claudius was the fifth Emperor, and this was the 9th imperial edict. It was passed in 51ad). This man and his wife would become important parts of the Battle for

Europe for Jesus Christ. They will eventually labor in various cities of New Testament note.

18.4 And he reasoned in the synagogue every sabbath, and persuaded the Jews and the Greeks.

18.4 in every Great War there is always a battle that turns the tide and momentum. The war will not be over but the eventual outcome is on the horizon. This was the case with Corinth in the spiritual battle for Europe. Corinth was a turning point. It was Satan's "Waterloo" so to speak. The march of the gospel of Jesus Christ through the Roman Empire was a foregone conclusion from this moment forward. Battles were still to be fought, but victory would never be doubted again. History now reflects that ten percent of the Roman Empire would become Christian in the next three hundred years. Corinth was the hinge that turned the triumph of the gospel into a rout for the gospel of Jesus Christ. The flame of the gospel burned across the Roman Empire like a prairie fire. The key to Satan's soft underbelly was discovered at Corinth. The key was the preaching of the gospel of Jesus Christ in it's most elemental form. Paul said And I, brethren, when I came to you, came not with excellency of speech or of wisdom, declaring unto you the testimony of God. For I determined not to know any thing among you, save Jesus Christ, and him crucified. *And I was with you in weakness, and in fear, and in much trembling. And my speech and my preaching was not with enticing words of man's wisdom, but in demonstration of the Spirit and of power:*

18.5-6 And when Silas and Timotheus were come from Macedonia, Paul was pressed in the spirit, and testified to the Jews that Jesus was Christ. 6 And when

they opposed themselves, and blasphemed, he shook his raiment, and said unto them, Your blood be upon your own heads; I am clean; from henceforth I will go unto the Gentiles.

18.5-6 Paul continued to the synagogue on the Sabbath and persuade the Jews and the Greeks. The coming of Silas and Timothy seemed to invigorate Paul and he was pressed in the spirit. Paul testified (protest earnestly), to the Jews. They strongly opposed Paul and his message so Paul departs from them. Paul determines to go unto the Gentiles. It appears Paul changes his venue from the synagogue to the house of Justus. It would appear this is where Crispus was converted. This simple move seemed to open the door to many conversions.

18.7-11 And he departed thence, and entered into a certain man's house, named Justus, one that worshipped God, whose house joined hard to the synagogue. 8 And Crispus, the chief ruler of the synagogue, believed on the Lord with all his house; and many of the Corinthians hearing believed, and were baptized. 9 Then spake the Lord to Paul in the night by a vision, Be not afraid, but speak, and hold not thy peace: 10 For I am with thee, and no man shall set on thee to hurt thee: for I have much people in this city. 11 And he continued there a year and six months, teaching the word of God among them.

18.7-11 The question remains' did this move from the synagogue to the house of Justus preempt the conversion of many Gentiles? God seems to put the divine seal of approval upon this move for it is at this juncture God speaks to Paul in a vision about the many people God has in the city of Corinth.

18.12-17 And when Gallio was the deputy of Achaia, the Jews made insurrection with one accord against Paul, and brought him to the judgment seat, 13 Saying, This fellow persuadeth men to worship God contrary to the law. 14 And when Paul was now about to open his mouth, Gallio said unto the Jews, If it were a matter of wrong or wicked lewdness, O ye Jews, reason would that I should bear with you: 15 But if it be a question of words and names, and of your law, look ye to it; for I will be no judge of such matters. 16 And he drave them from the judgment seat. 17 Then all the Greeks took Sosthenes, the chief ruler of the synagogue, and beat him before the judgment seat. And Gallio cared for none of those things.

18.12-17 The inclusion of the incident with Gallio is vintage Luke as the author. This attention to detail has been his signature style as the only Gentile writer of the New Testament. He is the most accurate with titles of officials, dates, and names of any author in the Bible. The Jewish religion was an approved religion by the Roman government and the new sect of Christianity was considered a form of Judaism. The Jews were attempting to strip Christianity away from the connection to their faith so they appeal to Gallio. The Roman official dismisses their appeal out of hand. The enraged Jews then beat Sosthenes the chief ruler of the synagogue as a protest. Paul grasps this opportunity to preach as well. Because this is happening at the Roman judgment seat of the proconsul, Paul later uses this image to present the judgment seat of Christ for a world awaiting judgment.

18.18 And Paul after this tarried there yet a good while, and then took his leave of the brethren, and sailed thence into Syria, and with him Priscilla and Aquila; having shorn his head in Cenchrea: for he had a vow.

18.18 Paul was there in Corinth for a great while longer. His inner spirit let Paul know it was time to continue the work God had sent him forth as an apostle to do. So with brevity, the Bible says he took his leave and sailed with Priscilla and Aquila for Syria. The greatest spiritual battle in the history of the world had been fought and won. Europe had been brought under the blood stained flag of Christianity. With five years behind him, and two missionary journeys, Paul was now a seasoned Apostle like the world had never before witnessed.

18.19-23 And he came to Ephesus, and left them there: but he himself entered into the synagogue, and reasoned with the Jews. 20 When they desired him to tarry longer time with them, he consented not; 21 But bade them farewell, saying, I must by all means keep this feast that cometh in Jerusalem: but I will return again unto you, if God will. And he sailed from Ephesus. 22 And when he had landed at Caesarea, and gone up, and saluted the church, he went down to Antioch. 23 And after he had spent some time there, he departed, and went over all the country of Galatia and Phrygia in order, strengthening all the disciples.

18.19-23 Ephesus was the famous city, capital of Ionia, and afterwards the scene of a large period of John's labors. It stood not far from the sea on some hilly ground by a small river which flows into the sea. In Paul's day it was by far the busiest and most populous city in Proconsular Asia. Paul leaves Aquila and Pricilla there and again enters the synagogue. Paul then travels to Caesarea, possibly to Philip the Evangelist's house (Acts 21.8). He then visits Antioch and confirms the disciples in Galatia and Phrygia. Note: In unimportant matters Paul was still amenable to Jewish customs and rites. His desire was to conciliate his Jewish opponents so far as he could without surrendering vital principles.

18.24-28 And a certain Jew named Apollos, born at Alexandria, an eloquent man, and mighty in the scriptures, came to Ephesus. 25 This man was instructed in the way of the Lord; and being fervent in the spirit, he spake and taught diligently the things of the Lord, knowing only the baptism of John. 26 And he began to speak boldly in the synagogue: whom when Aquila and Priscilla had heard, they took him unto them, and expounded unto him the way of God more perfectly. 27 And when he was disposed to pass into Achaia, the brethren wrote, exhorting the disciples to receive him: who, when he was come, helped them much which had believed through grace: 28 For he mightily convinced the Jews, and that publicly, shewing by the scriptures that Jesus was Christ.

18.24-28 Apollos; eloquent; the word in the original expresses not only ability as an orator, but also the possession of stores of learning. Hence the revised version gives learned. Either rendering only gives half the idea. He was learned and could use his learning with effect. Alexandria was a center of great study. The city was built under the direction of Dinocrates, the celebrated architect of the temple of Diana at Ephesus. It was there in Alexandria the Septuagint was compiled. As for Apollos, the study of the Old Testament flourished greatly in Alexandria, and Apollos had great power in the exposition and application of these Scriptures. The literary activity and philosophic pursuits of the Greek population of Alexandria were not without their effect on the more conservative Jews. We find from many sources that the Jewish writings were studied with all the literary exactness, which marked the Greek scholarship of the time. The Jews, conscious of the antiquity of their own records and yet impressed with the philosophic character of their cultured fellow-citizens, gave themselves greatly to the writings and the teachings of the schools. In study like this Apollos had no doubt been fully trained.

Note: the author Luke takes this point in the narrative to document Apollos contribution to the journey. Luke has already included Jesus, Paul, Aquila, Priscilla, Claudius, Silas, Timothy, Justus, Crispus, Gallio, Sosthenes, Apollos, and John the Baptist in this chapter. It is this attention to detail that has caused the skeptics of Holy scripture to remain silent. No other New Testament writer gives this attention to names and offices. Luke could not have known the scrutiny the Bible would experience over the next two millenniums, but the Holy Ghost was well aware and prompted Luke to be exacting.

The battle for Europe was not over but the victories were a roll call of New Testament churches. This three year period in New Testament history seems to be without parallel. From the day Paul had set foot on the continent of Europe until now there had been victories, defeats, hardships and challenges. From the first convert on the riverside at Philippi, to the journey back to Antioch, Paul had just completed the epic journey we now call his second missionary journey. Satan's bastions had been scaled and conquered. The banner of Jesus Christ proudly flew over the continent of Europe. Paul had indeed proven to be a chosen vessel.

www.ingramcontent.com/pod-product-compliance
Lightning Source LLC
Chambersburg PA
CBHW040325300426
44112CB00021B/2887